Robert Speir

Going south for the winter

With hints for consumptives

Robert Speir

Going south for the winter
With hints for consumptives

ISBN/EAN: 9783337257880

Printed in Europe, USA, Canada, Australia, Japan

Cover: Foto ©Lupo / pixelio.de

More available books at **www.hansebooks.com**

GOING SOUTH

FOR

THE WINTER.

WITH

HINTS FOR CONSUMPTIVES.

BY

ROBERT F. SPEIR, M. D.

NEW YORK:
PRINTED FOR THE AUTHOR
BY EDWARD O. JENKINS, 20 NORTH WILLIAM STREET.
1870.

Entered according to Act of Congress, in the year 1869, by
ROBERT F. SPEIR, M. D.,
In the Clerk's Office of the District Court of the United States for the Eastern District of New York.

CONTENTS.

Preface,	5
Pulmonary Consumption,	9
Who Suffer Most,	10
Primary Cause of Pulmonary Phthisis,	12
Atmospheric Vicissitudes,	17
Climatic Influences,	25
Going Off,	33
How to Go,	34
Savannah, Georgia,	35
The Other Route,	37
Charleston,	38
Jacksonville,	41
Mandarin,	45
Magnolia,	45
Hibernia,	46
Green Cove Spring,	47
Pilatka,	51

Contents.

St. Augustine, Florida,
Enterprise,
Lake Harney,
Aiken, South Carolina,
South of France,
Diet,
Exercise
Stimulants,
Sea-Bathing,
Conclusion,

PREFACE.

VERY few physicians have had the time or opportunity to inform themselves of the advantages of climatic influences in the treatment of phthisis pulmonalis by personal observation in the South. And notwithstanding the fact that the physician has the interest of his patient ever so much at heart, and does his duty conscientiously, never having seen the country, it is difficult to designate any particular locality "down South" as the best suited for his consumptive patient.

From the general confusion and diversity of opinion existing in the minds of so many persons with defective breathing apparatus, who so anxiously seek advice about wintering in the South, and partly by persuasion, and for the information of those who cannot spare the time to investigate for themselves, I have after a late extended experimental tour, and careful observation while wintering in the South, with *a view to ascertain* the medicinal qualities, humidity, density and dryness of the air, prepared this *little hand-book* as my contribution to the general fund of information most to be desired, and so little known by the thousands of consumptives who are ignorant of everything but the terrible truth that they *must do something*.

In this little treatise the writer would desire not to be misunderstood as offering any direct advice to his readers, but only in as few words as possible, simply present a condition of things which he does not remember ever to have seen presented for the consideration of those northern consumptives who are "going South for the winter."

The writer would hope to present the facts

only (having no interest in hotels, or orange-groves and land speculations), so that his readers can judge of their destination understandingly for themselves.

A small part of these "notes" from the writer, first appeared in the *Medical and Surgical Reporter*.

ROBERT F. SPEIR, M. D.

Montague Place,
Brooklyn Heights, N. Y., 1870.

Going South for the Winter.

PULMONARY CONSUMPTION.

Pulmonary consumption is a disease common to the whole human race, and apparently to animals as well. This dreaded disease may prevail in the high lands, where the air is dry; and in the low lands, where the air is moist. It is not contagious, and cannot be transferred from man to man. The disease is known to lie latent for a long period, while there are no declared symptoms of its existence till it breaks out with a suddenness that is startling.

The mortality from pulmonary consumption is frightful, and it is not surprising that the disease should be thus mortal, when the treatment pursued is everything but what it should be. But the fact is now fully recognized, and there is no longer a doubt or want of proof that the progress of the disease may be permanently arrested, and life once more made bearable by the happy results of good treatment; but, because there are not a few cases of pulmomary consumption where the tubercles heal up, leaving a cicatrix, just as an external wound, it must not, however, be supposed the disease will yield without the most persistent effort to keep it under control. Neither should the consumptive invalid be too hopeful, for at any time a little imprudence, exposure or overexertion, may renew the trouble, defy all treatment, and rapidly prove fatal.

WHO SUFFER MOST.

Visit where you may the winter resorts of consumptive invalids, and you will have ample evidence to establish the proof that, it is our young men and women, the life and hope of the country, who suffer most severely from attacks of this terrible disease. If this distressing statement so often reiterated, be true is it not a matter of such consequence as to demand particular attention? Yet we come in contact daily with persons presenting every symptom of serious lung disease, who will not even make an effort, or attempt to avert the danger of phthisis. And strange as it may seem, there are people who will not take as a warning the sad picture of the once blooming girl, lately so happy and joyous, now fading from an attack of consumption; threatening to drag her—perhaps the only hope and pride of her unhappy parents, and the joy of her friends and admirers—to an early grave.

We daily meet with people who are so blind as not to see in the flushed cheek, emaciation and teasing cough of their young friend, the life of all his associates, a cause for fearful apprehensions. And it is often useless to advise such deluded people, for so flattering and insidious is the character of pulmonary disease, that your anxious warnings may be received without attention.

Of the thousands of consumptives "going South" for the winter, many have only reached maturity, to find instead of the strength and vitality natural to manhood, only sufficient cause to repent a broken-down constitution, a burden to themselves and their friends.

PRIMARY CAUSE OF PULMONARY PHTHISIS.

Of all the transparent acts of folly a parent can be guilty of, there is none so inexcusable as that self-delusion and willful pride which induces the parent or guardian to put upon a child the most unreasonable and trying mental exercises, while perfectly regardless of the physical development.

Can any or all of the so-called accomplishments and empty honors, compensate for the shattered nervous system, dyspepsia, ruined eye-sight and destructive development of brain, at the risk of making the child prematurely old and physically ruined.

Witness those darlings who astonish us by their early performances. Did it ever occur to you that the bright little girl, with her palid cheek, and those lustrous large eyes, who is complimented by foolish friends to please the vanity of the parent, is sure to become another sacrifice. The little six-year-old is admired and caressed for his astonishing precocity, encouraged and flattered while the little fellow works away, growing paler and thinner, and finally the bright and beautiful boy *has a cough,* and is soon laid in his silent grave, beside hundreds of little victims of parental ambition. It must be clear to every mind that many of those little curly-headed prattlers, whose innocent voices are hushed in their untimely graves, might have been saved. It surely is not prudent or wise to overtax the powers of the young child, or generous to push him beyond his years. Why not let him live in the enjoyment of a life nature marked out for him.

It is enough to drive one mad to see the little creatures returning home from school with an armful of books and pages to ponder over, which would puzzle a strong man to wade through.

We hear of school commissions and the promotion of teachers who secure their elevation by the prompt manner in which the children of their department are "put through" with their studies, while the children are really so confined at school that every mouthful of air respired is loaded with the poison from the lungs of another. Is it any wonder that these children—those who live to reach maturity—discover too late the ravages of confirmed pulmonary consumption? Among all the short-sightedness which regard the education of the youth, this insane effort to over-stimulate the child in mental tasks is the source of the greatest mischief to defective lungs; and if you would know the result of this criminal cramming of weakly children, go count the little mounds in your cemetery. It is beautifully said, we go out of the world by the same changes almost as those by which we enter it. We begin as children—as children we leave off. We return at last to the same weak and helpless condition as our first. We must have people to lift us, to carry us, to provide nourishment and even to feed us. We again have need of parents; and how wise the provision. We find them again in our children, who now take delight in repaying a part of that kindness which we showed them. Children now step in, as it were, into the place of parents. While our weakness transposes us into the place of children, why, then, annihilate the children?

Another exciting cause of pulmonary disease is the destructive perpetual motion, prolonged irritation and artificial life so characteristic of our irrepressible American people, particularly the young. When our people will persist in despising the dictates of nature and indulge in excesses that *must develop* disease, while keeping up a continual ruinous, physical and mental activity, giving brain and muscle no time for rest, driving ahead like a drove of sheep, how *can* such people expect to escape diseases of the vital organs? Every well-informed person knows that these nervous, excitable, fidgety, fussy, bustling, awfully-efficient, restless spirits, with not a moment for reflection or repose, and without exercising the slightest deliberation or discrimination in eating, *must* hereafter suffer for such imprudence. Another active cause of consumption (among females) is undue lactation. Few mothers have the constitutional vigor required to nurse the infant an unusual number of months. Many cases of lung trouble derive their origin from reckless exposure at late hours of the night without suitable clothing, especially under-wear, to protect the body from chill when over-warm and cooling rapidly, arresting the functions of the skin, and forcing upon the circulation the work for the pores of the skin. No reasonable man will follow the popular notion that one becomes hardy by exposure to cold. Those children are fortunate, indeed, whose guardians do not strip their little legs of every covering in their earliest childhood, laying the foundation for pulmonary trouble.

ATMOSPHERIC VICISSITUDES.

Consumptive people are especially alive to the fact that the *kind* of air they breathe has a more or less exciting and controlling influence over the frequency and depth of their respiration.

In breathing the foul air escaped from decayed compounds of garbage of the streets, or the confined air, pulverized dust and emanations from the body, floated in the atmosphere of lecture-rooms or a crowded ball-room, with its hundreds of maddened, flying, human beings, the consumptive suffers immediately from a decided clogging of the respiratory apparatus. The respiration becomes labored, the difficulty increasing till there is complete aeration of the blood by a fresh supply of oxygen. Again, if the air contained more than the natural proportion of oxygen, we could not breathe it; its stimulating effect upon the respiratory movements are such as to endanger life.

The air of the atmosphere is productive of

such a variety of effects upon the condition of the consumptive invalid, that it cannot be overlooked in the treatment of phthisis. Ask a schoolboy to define atmosphere, and he will tell you that it is a thin, transparent, invisible fluid which surrounds us, and reaches above us about forty miles. He will tell you that atmospheric air is known to be composed of, at least, two kinds of air—the one called oxygen, the other nitrogen gas.

Oxygen gas is our great agent in respiration, while the purity of the air we breathe must depend upon the proportion of oxygen in the atmosphere—the proper proportion of these two parts of the air being, as supposed, about twenty-six parts oxygen and seventy-three of nitrogen, with the small quantity of hydrogen and carbonic acid gas. With a view to ascertain the medicinal qualities of the air, many inferences from speculations and experiments have been made, but without any very satisfactory results. We have instruments for measuring and testing the air, but not much has been done of practical value to the consumptive. But we have a daily accumulation of unmistakable evidence, that for the consumptive to visit public places of amusement and ball-rooms, and breathe such an irritating atmosphere, as for hours they must do, is surely to peril life, by exhausting what little vitality remains, sending them to their lodgings with increased respirations, pale face and flushing of the cheeks, to pass a restless night, accompanied with incessant coughing and sweating, till overcome by complete prostration. We are told that in two hours one hundred persons will render unfit for respiration one thousand feet of cubic air of a lecture-hall, and that each gas jet produces as much poisonous air as four persons.

Professor Ganot, in his experiments, assures us of what amount of pressure we bear from the atmosphere. He says: " Considering the surface of a man of fair size to be about twelve square feet, the weight which the man supports on the surface of his body is upwards of eleven tons. Such an enormous pressure might seem impossible to be borne; but it must be remembered that in all directions there are equal and contrary pressure which counterbalance one another. It might be supposed," he says, "that the effect of this force of air, acting in all directions, would be to press the body together and crush it; but the solid parts of the skeleton could resist a far higher pressure; and as the air and liquids contained in the organs and vessels, the air having the same density as the external air, cannot be further compressed by atmospheric air."

The pressure from within is easily seen by the distension of the surface when the external pressure is removed from any part of the body by the air-pump. Now, as we are able, to a certain degree, to determine the physical and medicinal qualities of the air, we can form a pretty clear judgment of the dryness, humidity and effects of air on the condition of the consumptive.

Every intelligent person knows how thoroughly vegetable and animal poisons impregnate the air; and it is just as well known that certain localities are noted for the frequency of fevers; another as the certain source of diarrheal diseases; another as fostering and encouraging disease of the throat and lungs, with asthmatic difficulty; another region is, perhaps, prominent for endemic and epidemic visitations, all conveyed "on the wings of the wind." Much of the wide-spread diseases of the chest is to be directly traced to the poison in the air.

It is considered that the air of the higher situation is more pure than that of the lower country; but Hufeland says, "the greatest degree of height, the glaciers, is prejudicial to health, and Switzerland, the highest land in Europe, has produced fewer instances of longevity than Scotland."

The only explanation we have for this is, that the atmosphere is too dry, ethereal and pure, and therefore consumes more quickly, which is unfavorable to duration of life.

Uniformity in the condition of the atmosphere, particularly in regard to heat and cold, is what we most desire for the consumptive, who should avoid, if possible, localities where great and sudden variations of barometer and thermometer are usual. While all extremes, either too much or too little, too high or too low, are necessarily dangerous for persons with weak lungs.

A situation subject to a continual mixture of heat and cold, where one experiences often in the course of the day March and July weather, is dangerous to pulmonary patients. To consumptives, a very high degree of dryness of the air, as well as too great moisture, are alike unfavorable. It is said moist air, being already saturated, has less attractive power over bodies — that it consumes them less. We know that in a moist atmosphere there is always more uniformity of temperature, and an atmosphere somewhat moist is supposed to keep the organs longer pliable; whereas that which is too dry brings on much sooner aridity of the vessels, and all the characteristics of old age. Hufeland says, "In islands mankind always become older than in continents lying under the same latitude; that men live longer in the islands of the Archipelago than in the neighboring countries of Asia, in Cyprus than in Syria, in Japan than China, and in England than Germany."

The consumptive can have no vitality or healthy circulation of the blood without the lungs, heart, brain and stomach perform their work *with energy.* Cramming with nourishment, without complete oxygenation of the blood, will not accomplish the work.

The consumptive must be surrounded with, and breathe in a pure atmosphere; but the habit of exposing oneself to a draught or stream of cold air is not to be indulged. All the refreshing, restorative and invigorating influences of the air can be had without the careless exposure and letting down of the sash of every window in the apartment, making the admission of fresh air almost fatal to the pulmonary invalid.

The offensive and dangerous air of a close room, so destructive to the rapid improvement of the consumptive can find its escape by other and better outlets. The *open fire-*

place, and the improved ventilator, which should be attached to every sick-room, and which no house can be complete without.

It is a lamentable fact that so many friends, having the care of the sick, do not at all appreciate the advantages of a well-ventilated sick-room, with all the appliances and conveniences that science, kindness and common sense would dictate. Such an apartment should be complete in all the appurtenances of a luxurious sick-room. When not required for an invalid; the rooms could always be used as the *much-needed* apartment for stealing a little quiet forgetfulness and plenteous repose, at a time when, in every other room in the house, one cannot sleep without being liable to be disturbed, *just* when to be disturbed is to make one furious.

Many persons have a confused notion of how much fresh air is required to fill a sick-room, as well as how to provide an escape for the noxious gases. An open window is not always a safe method of ventilation. The vicious, confined air of a sick-room is always ascending to the ceiling, and there coming in contact with the cool wall is condensed, becomes heavier, and falls along the side of the wall to the floor, where it *should* find its proper escape at an open fire-place, and not at the window.

CLIMATIC INFLUENCES.

While there is no longer a doubt or want of proof of a successful treatment of phthisis pulmonalis, *there is a doubt* of the climatic influences, all things considered, best suited to phthisis cases; and as there is no disease so certainly anticipated and influenced by climatic changes, the question becomes one of the utmost importance for the consideration of the consumptive. If life is to be shortened by remaining North in the winter, or health secured and life prolonged by "going South for the winter," then, of course, there can be no choice for the consumptive. When *we know* that as many as twenty thousand northern pulmonary invalids passed through Richmond, Charleston and Savannah on their way South during every winter since the late "unpleasantness," it will be seen that it is an important question, whether these thousands who endure all the discomforts and privations incident thereto realize the improvement so anxiously sought, or can the expenditure of money, time, patience and strength be saved with a prospect of renewal of health without "going South for the winter." It is certainly the most refined cruelty to send the poor consumptives so far from home and friends, hurried off in an apparently helpless condition, unless fully informed of their destination and discomforts awaiting them. It is a sad state that in which you find many unfortunate northern consumptives in the South during the winter months. Too many are ordered or advised to go "down South" often without the slightest intelligent preparation, without the most simple but necessary comforts provided, totally uninformed of where they are to go or how to get there. Some there are who go South in the winter for amusement, leaving home in perfect health, and who readily find everything "couleur de rose," securing so-called comforts and accommodations which, to our poor, suffering invalid would simply be outrageous and dangerous trifling. Consumptive invalids need comforts, attention, sympathy and encouragement, and cannot be expected to join with the hearty travellers in the pell-mell rush for steamboat, stage, state-room, hotel register and sleeping-car. Many consumptives who reach Florida alive are often in a most painfully distressing state—low spirited, far away from home, discouraged and among strangers, their sufferings cannot well be imagined. Sent from home on a forlorn hope, too many of these poor wandering people only reach their destination and die.

Wintering in the South, particularly Eastern Florida, which is so often alluded to for the supposed curative influence of the atmosphere, is attended with some difficulties and privations which it is well for the consumptive to consider before going South. All considerations of climate must be comparative. The alternations of heat and cold cannot, even in Florida, be relied upon entirely. The climate, generally so delicious in winter, will, at times, conduct itself like a wayward child, while the incapacity of the hotel-keepers, want of attention to guests, and manner of preparing food, which is often perfectly innutritious and but poorly cooked, so different from what the consumptive is accustomed to at home, that he early *loses all relish* for anything placed before him, and the consequence is the body is never well nourished.

It would, therefore, prove a weak and foolish act for consumptive people to go to Florida, or elsewhere South, in search of health, while they are entirely unacquainted with the nature of the country,—the temperature, contagious miasmata, atmospheric vicissitudes, elevation, dryness or humidity, and quality of the diet and drinking water.

They might find, instead of the cool draughts of sweet pure water in their northern springs, only the most nauseous pond and lake water of abominable taste and qualities, and often without a particle of ice to settle the mud in the drinking vessels; perhaps, instead of the refreshing breeze so grateful to the parched and feverish consumptive, only the most suffocating air. They might find no frost or snow, but instead, the heat of the sun at meridian pouring its unpitying rays upon an already weakened frame; and the heavy dews at night, not at all what they were led to expect by the exaggerated reports of interested and inconsiderate parties. They might discover that to obtain a nourishing and palatable diet was attended with uncontrollable difficulties, and often impossible.

It is easy for people who are strong and hearty, and who can devour everything before them greedily, to say that the hotel-keepers do really seem to do their best for their guests, and it won't do to be too hard on them; but my inquiries and experiments in Florida were not made with reference to *such* people, but *entirely* with an eye to the interest of the suffering consumptive, and those sportsmen who so boastfully talk of the splendid entertainment they receive are not to be considered in this treatise. I am sure I care nothing for the interest and success of the hotel adventurers, who "run" their hotels as if their guests had no rights, which hotel-men are bound to respect, and who are many times so regardless of the comfort of those unfortunately sick thrown in their way, being indifferent to everything but skill in packing the greatest number of invalids in the smallest possible space at three and four dollars per day. This packing system in Florida is pushed with systematic vigor; and as for beds, it were easier to stand up and sleep. Those stupid and deluded people who are so simple as to imagine they are well provided for at a Florida hotel only excite my pity. *The consumptive must have always and everywhere a regular systematic and nutritious diet, and a rousing, restoring heroic treatment,* and how to get it for the winter in the South is the question.

The climate of Florida in the winter is

Going South for the Winter. 31

generally most delightfully warm with glorious sunshine and without frost, but to obtain anything more, the most simple food and miserable accommodation, in the present state of things, is very difficult. The hotels must depend, for their uncertain supplies, upon the St. John river steamers from the North. A person in health can enjoy the winter and live well (for him) while shooting and fishing, but the pulmonary invalid, accustomed to the delicacies and comforts at home, cannot get food of a sufficiently nutritive, palatable and supporting character. Such articles of diet, as fine fresh butter, rich cream, fat beef and lamb, strong hearty animal food, which is of the greatest consequence, and which the consumptive *must* have if he would improve his distressed condition, he cannot get.

Parties who go to East Florida with the stupid idea that they will buy the needful delicacies, will find, on "interviewing" the freedman, that greenbacks are not sufficient inducement to persuade the colored man to shoot and fish *for anybody*. While the continuous lakes that make up the St. John's river are alive with fine fish, jumping from the water in every direction and easily taken; if the verdant invalid beg the native to catch some fish for him, he will probably tell you, "No use gwyne to dar riber, cause the gud durn fish don't bite dar, sho' as you live, boss."

The innocent delight of the Florida "fifteenth amendment" is to sleep, eat bacon, and keep "shady" whenever he can; so that the pulmonary invalid from the North must go without his fresh fish, or paddle his own canoe and hunt and fish for himself, which is impossible.

From the difficulty of receiving supplies from the North in good order in Florida, the regulation of the diet, an *essential point*, cannot be properly attended to at the hotels, now the winter resorts of the army of northern invalids. Consumptive people *may* be improved on the hog and hominy diet, but I have not happened to fall in with any who looked as if they had *been improved*. Florida does not produce good beef, mutton, or milk, all of which are positively necessary for making up a diet for the consumptive.

"GOING OFF."

No one who may be suffering from pulmonary consumption should venture to leave the comforts, sympathy, attention, nutritious diet and encouragement to be found at home among friends, and go "South for the winter," without having made the most ample and liberal preparation.

The question *of going*, and *where to go*, should be well discussed, and, when decided, *go direct* to the point selected, without loitering about with careless indifference concerning your movements.

There is generally great depression, uneasiness, and often complete breaking down of the unfortunate consumptive, when "Going Off." While the dread of leaving friends and loved relations, perhaps, for the last time, is very touching, and altogether indescribable, many times producing serious nervous prostrations, which cannot but be dangerous to the consumptive.

This should not be encouraged, but wisely provided for when friends are
"Going South for the winter."

"HOW TO GO."

In "going South for the winter," the invalid has a choice of route; parties who do not suffer from sea-sickness, will find the steamers leaving New York several times a week, the most desirable conveyance, provided the invalid can be assured of any positive comfort in a sea voyage, cooped up in the close cabin, and after, pounded to a jelly almost, from rolling in the berth of a state-room.

Most invalids who suffer from phthisis in "going South for the winter," should take the safe and easy route from New York to Philadelphia, ninety miles, by rail, remain over one or two days at Philadelphia; then from Philadelphia, (stop at Baltimore), to Washington, one hundred and thirty-six miles, by rail; again, leave Washington for Richmond, (stop at Wilmington), one hundred and thirty miles, by rail; a few days at Richmond for repose and renewed strength, and then off for Augusta, Georgia, when the consumptive will be wise if he stop a while, en route. Many consumptives would find it profitable and healthful to remove to Augusta permanently, perhaps. At all events, to winter here is worth a trial. The city of Augusta is a handsome and thriving place, very like a northern city, and more pleasing in appearance to the eye of a northern man than any city south of Baltimore. The changes of temperature are sometimes sudden, however, and March winds rather trying. Having decided to leave Augusta, you may take the roomy sleeping-car for Savannah.

SAVANNAH, GEORGIA.

Savannah is the largest city of Georgia, and very beautifully laid out. Streets generally unpaved, but all handsomely shaded by the charming Melia Azedarach (Pride of India) trees. There are the most lovely little squares or parks all over the city, in all, about twenty or thirty, lined with lofty shade trees. Opposite the "Pulaski House," on the square, is a noble monument erected in memory of Gen. Pulaski. The luxuriance of the growth, and the freshness of the out-door creeping vines and shrubs, add much to the appearance of the city. The wonderful cemetery of Bonaventre is a great curiosity to the stranger. A week spent here at the "Pulaski," or "Skreven House" will give the consumptive invalid an opportunity to renew his strength, and eat the *last good meal* he may expect till returned from Florida.

The drinking water of the city is poor and even dangerous to some persons who use it for the first time. The writer would not be doing his duty if he neglected to warn strangers against indulging freely in the drinking water of Savannah, and, in fact, all the drinking water after leaving Charleston to go South, should be used with caution. The consumptive has more to fear from a violent diarrhea, brought about by the unhealthy water everywhere south of Charleston, than he can imagine. The writer *knows* of what he speaks, having *seen and felt* the effects of drinking this water, in his own, and a number of other cases of northern people who go South.

The city of Savannah, with its great, noble old trees, wide streets, neat well-kept parks and abundance of shade, has more the appearance of a great county town, than the busy commercial city that it is. The winters are very mild and the atmosphere easy to breathe, but generally pretty well charged with moisture.

THE OTHER ROUTE.

The invalid who is seriously ill, and is desirous of going *through to Florida* without stopping, would find that a very difficult matter to accomplish by rail, as the cars do not connect as promptly as they should. A sleeping-car could be taken at New York through to Richmond, and again sleeping-car to Augusta and Charleston.

To go by steamer to Charleston is the most direct, if the patient can weather a sea-voyage in winter; then from Charleston to Savannah and Jacksonville, by the "inside" route; making the outside sea-trip only that from New York to Charleston.

CHARLESTON.

A few days at Charleston will not be lost to the invalid; and this city, as a home for the winter, will suit a class of consumptives who *must be* in regular and easy communication with the Eastern States.

The inducements for remaining at Charleston a short time for a trial of the air, before going to Florida, are many. The city always has a warm, cheerful look; with its streets lined with ornamental trees, tasty gardens and profusion of shrubbery and climbing vines enclosing the neatly painted piazzas, all combining to remind the stranger of spring and summer at home.

The houses—many of them are of elegant and solid proportions. The streets are well and widely laid out—though now need paving again—with the stones removed from the streets to fill up a wall for Fort Sumter during the war. The business part of the city—on which are the warehouses and shops—present always a lively, busy scene. The stores are well supplied with French and English goods. Many of the wealthy residents who suffered so severely during the late war, and who still occupy the best dwellings, are to be seen daily out among the well-dressed crowd; and easily recognized by their dignified manner and characteristic style. Some of the best houses are yet in a dilapidated condition, having a forlorn, deserted look, as if they were frowning down upon the spot from whence Gilmore and his swamp-angel sent so many unwelcome messages.

Charleston has some excellent hotels, which are *the* attraction always for the stranger in a strange place. The "Mills House" is a stately building, and pleasantly situated. The old popular resort, the "Charleston House," is much in the style of "Barnum's Hotel" of Baltimore; and is a most comfortable, roomy, old-fashioned hotel; the rooms are large and airy. In this city and neighborhood are "sights" enough to amuse the invalid for a few days while resting, before taking the steamer to Savannah. Fort Sumter, Magnolia Cemetery, Castle Pinckney, the old Customhouse, where our revolutionary patriots were held by the British, are, with many public buildings and private residences, worth seeing. The time can be agreeably employed in a variety of beautiful drives in the immediate vicinity of the city. Charleston has some fine club-houses, restaurants, and excellent Mill Pond oysters. Theatres and places of amusement are not numerous, or very well supported. There is little sociability, except among the middle-class of society. The old South Carolinians are very reserved, and proudly claim a superiority—former elegance

Going South for the Winter. 41

and lavish luxury—which will not permit them to visit only in their own circle. It would be difficult to find a better place, or more comfortable hotel to stop at and luxuriate a little before "going to Florida for the winter."

JACKSONVILLE.

The town—or rather as the inhabitants love to call it—city of Jacksonville, stretches along the west side of the river St. John, and back into the country a considerable distance. This town, with a harbor so spacious that ocean vessels of a thousand tons can come up the river to the landing, and a population consisting now mostly of New England people, is destined to be the great business centre of Florida. The climate is balmy, and remarkably soothing; with cool nights, such as to make it necessary to have a good fire after sun-set, as a safe-guard against fevers. The buildings are extremely old-fashioned, and of irregular style, wanting paint badly; and now either whitewashed, or entirely neglected, presenting a faded, dreary appearance. The soil is very light; and in order to make the streets passable for pedestrians, each side of the main streets is paved with plank, which answers pretty well for a footpath.

The chief attraction for northern people to go to Jacksonville to locate permanently, is the peculiar climate, cheapness of land, (two or three dollars per acre,) and opportunities for market gardening, which is largely entered into by Eastern States people all along the river. There is much activity and business energy exhibited by the people, and the profits of market gardening, with frequent opportunities for shipping North from here, will make Jacksonville a very busy place. A number of store-houses and neat cottages have recently been erected, and the grounds attached to the new houses are all prettily laid out, with walks and shrubs and the greatest variety of flowers, which can be cultivated and bloom all winter. The character and appearance of Jacksonville is being changed and modernized. In fact, the whole town is being

Going South for the Winter. 43

rebuilt and made a New England town. A large hotel, called the St. James, capable of accommodating comfortably one hundred or more guests, is now open, has a good situation, a few moments' walk from the landing. The other hotels have been longer built, but are good enough of their kind. There are any number of private boarding-houses, which will receive parties to board for the winter, and one would think there was room enough for all who wished to remain at Jacksonville for a trial of the air, before going further South on the river. Still, many invalids who arrive here in urgent need of nice comfortable quarters, are frequently compelled to put up with quite inferior apartments.

The rush to Jacksonville is often so great, that if the whole population of the town should turn out, their houses would not furnish room for the army of consumptives who have found their way here. There are *a few cows* to be found here, but *un-skimmed* milk, fresh eggs, and good butter are very scarce, and command high prices. The charges for board, at all the winter resorts of invalids who go to Florida, is about what you pay at any of our northern summer resorts, but rooms can sometimes be had by parties of three or four, who furnish their own table, and, perhaps, board at a low price, can be had in some hotels and boarding-houses; but, *good board*, a *generous table*, attendance, and such fare as the consumptive *must positively have*, will cost three, four, and five dollars per day. The most decided indifference as to what quantity and quality of food is supplied for the consumptive, is remarked at all the stopping places in Florida. The expenses are large, and the trouble of keeping a good supply of fresh meats in such a climate, makes all hotel people keep an eye to the profits,—their "season" being only for three months. There is daily communication with the North from Jacksonville, by rail and boat. Steamers from this town are daily ascending and descending the river, while, often the consumptive will have more comfort and better table on the steamers "City Point," and "Lizzie Baker," or "Dictator," than can be had on the shores at boarding-houses; but, anywhere and everywhere, *the fare* is poor, and *not* suited to the condition of the worn-out famished sufferer, with lung disease.

MANDARIN.

Going South from Jacksonville on the steamer "Dictator," you soon come in sight of a rickety old pier, fronting a point of land called Mandarin, a most uninviting, gloomy place to live, one would say. This spot is marked by all invalids going on the river St. John, and by *all Southerners*, from the fact of Mrs. Stowe being the owner of everything there worth having, including an orange grove of great promise.

MAGNOLIA.

Dr. Benedict, of St. Augustine, was the first to take advantage of this "opening," and at one time had a flourishing establishment here, which has passed out of his hands, and the Dr. resumed practice in St. Augustine. The hotel is still open, and guests receive all the attention and comfort possible to have in this region. The steamers on the St. John all touch at Magnolia, and a number of northern consumptives stop for the winter. The hotel, as in fact are nearly all on the river, is kept by Eastern States people. It is not unusual to meet with invalids in Florida who are very happy about their improvement at Magnolia. It will not, perhaps, damage the consumptive much, after once on the St. John river, to give all these places a temporary trial. It won't do for a sick man to lose his senses, and rashly give up all hope of benefit without a trial.

HIBERNIA.

A good place, surely, for a hearty party of sportsmen to bivouac. Hibernia has the same features in common with all other places on the river. When a steamer touches the landing here, there is always some poor consumptive creature leaving the boat to find his way to the little hotel, not knowing or caring why, often. The languid indifference of these wretched people, ignorantly wandering about in search of health, reminds one òf the goneness and lost personality of a man thoroughly sea-sick. The only change and pastime the unfortunates have while here, is to get down to the landing on the arrival of every boat, and, with their upturned faces, watch each passenger in the hope of seeing a familiar face from the cold North; and the delight and satisfaction on seeing some consumptive acquaintance come off the plank is wonderful, even though they wish no one ill. Still misery loves company.

GREEN COVE SPRING.

At a landing called Green Cove Spring, you find you are over one hundred miles south of Jacksonville on the St. John river. Here there is one hotel and several good private boarding-houses. Captain Glinski and Captain Henderson, old residents, have a select number of guests in their private houses during the winter, and if the invalid must go to this place, it is wise to get accommodations at either of these two private boarding-houses. A multitude of consumptive and rheumatically-disposed people go to Green Cove Spring, and many land without finding any decent accommodation whatever. The only hotel is generally crowded when the boat reaches the pier; and I hope my readers may never see the distressing sight of such poor exhausted invalids as one will see dragging their weary limbs over this long pier to the hotel, to have only the pleasing intelligence that "if you will room with a *nice party* on the top floor *now*, I can do better by and by." And this is repeated day after day, all winter, through the whole of Florida.

The writer was glad to find shelter, and delighted on being favored even with a comfortable bed on the floor of the parlor of the hotel, he making one of four *compagnons de voyage*, three being just arrived from the cold

North, without scarce a spark of life left them. The parlor, smoking-room and every vacant spot in-doors, is used to "stow away" the sufferers. The parlor being the poorest place for the invalid to be booked for, as he must "stop up" till the room is left by the guests of the house. This will apply to all resorts now so crowded by northern invalids in search of health.

Excepting during a few days in winter, the climate is delightful—but not stimulating or tonic in the least—quite warm in the day-time, and, for some, almost debilitating. The sulphur spring is resorted to by persons suffering from rheumatism and dyspepsia, who think they get benefited. The spring consists of a basin about fifty feet across, inclosed by undergrowth completely, so that bathers who use the water have the privilege to bathe without the vexation of using a close bathing-room—rather a primitive style—but where all are so dreadfully sick, it is not considered necessary to be too nice about appearances. It is understood among those who frequent this pool of sulphur water that there are days reserved for females to enjoy the water exclusively.

A beautiful leaping cascade is formed from the waste water of the spring, and the water is always strongly impregnated with sulphur, which is gulped down by many enthusiasts. At this resort, beautiful enough by nature, you experience the same difficulty as elsewhere in Florida—the serious want of *ice, good drinking water*, milk and strong rich food. There is a want of appetite and a relaxed feeling, without the bracing air of the North (cold as it is), to give tone to the system and life to the blood. Under the most favorable circumstances, perhaps, some consumptives could winter here and possibly improve.

It should be *positively understood* between the party "going South for the winter" and parties who engage to furnish apartments and proper board for the consumptive invalid, that no mistake is made. It is generally impossible to secure good accommodations on the *arrival* of the steamer at any of these landings in Florida, unless engaged before, and often not even then. Hotel-men are quite indifferent about the matter.

PILATKA.

This is the most agreeable place the consumptive will meet on the river St. John. This little village, with a half dozen country stores, a hotel, good drug-store, two churches and a newspaper, is the only live place after leaving Jacksonville. Pleasant cottages are here and there springing up to help the appearance of the place.

The river boats all stop at this landing, affording constant communication between this place and Savannah. Mr. Austin, from one of the Eastern States, keeps a very comfortable hotel, and provides as good a table as at any other point on the river. A new hotel, well kept, well provided and well supplied with such comforts and luxuries as consumptives need, and suffer without, would, if established here, *pay* beyond anything a hotel-speculator could imagine.

The village is situated upon the most rising ground on the river. The stores all have a good supply of northern goods. The air is pure and soothing to pulmonary irritations, with a clear sky and abundance of sunshine—that great source of human joy and friend of the consumptive. The writer was struck with the evident opportunity offered, and the wisdom and advantage to persons suffering from pulmonary consumption, to organize and leave home in a company, with servants, nurse and a good supply of comforts and conveniences, to locate here for the winter, sending forward temporary cottages, shipped and put up ready to receive them. In this way all the necessary provisions could be made for a comfortable winter, while orders could be held for luxuries, knick-knacks, meats and delicacies regularly from the North. There are enough consumptives who can "join in," after reaching Florida, and pursue this course. Tomatoes, green peas, radishes and lettuce, with early potatoes, can be grown as early as March.

ST. AUGUSTINE, FLORIDA.

St. Augustine we know to be the oldest settled place in the United States. The old friend of Columbus was the first to visit the coast, and named it Florida, from the great number and variety of flowers. The little settlement of St. Augustine was at one time completely sacked and plundered by an English pirate who found his way here. In 1640 there was a population of two thousand persons, who made up a thrifty little village. General Jackson forced the Spanish to lower their standard to the Stars and Stripes, after a Spanish rule of two hundred years. General Jackson never spared his men in this Florida war— marching them hundreds of miles in the shortest possible time.

A Spanish captain brought to the settlement of St. Augustine as early as 1690 a lot of Spanish negroes to work his plantation; hence the early inauguration of slavery. St. Augustine has more to recommend it as a winter residence for persons suffering from diseases of the chest than any other spot in Florida. The climate is extremely mild and lovely, with strong tonic sea-air. Many wealthy people, who do not care to risk the extreme variations of temperature of our Northern States, have fled from a cold home in the North, purchased land and erected comfortable cottages here, for living during the winter, free from snow and eternal ice. For those consumptives who are recommended *sea-air* with mild climate, St. Augustine, in full view of the glorious ocean, lashing and rolling heavily on the most beautiful shores, is unsurpassed as a winter home. The distressed consumptive, when here, is not so likely to suffer from the extreme languor and complete exhaustion, so common to persons with phthisis. The sea-breeze is most refreshing and invigorating to these feverish invalids.

On rising of a morning, after a good night's rest, to find the warm morning sun shining brightly through your window is more cheering and reviving than the feeling of disappointment on looking from your padded sick-room out upon the snow-covered streets in the North.

This old town is the only really favored spot to winter in this whole flat, miserable, marshy country. The town is less than ten feet above the sea, and the Government constructed an extensive wall to protect the place from the encroachments of the sea (imperfections in this wall will sometime wake the inhabitants rather early of a morning). This great wall was from 1837 to 1848 in building. The strangers who spend the winter here find this wall a grand promenade of a moonlight night, with the ocean bounding in upon one, till stayed by the granite wall at your feet.

The United States band from the Barracks affords about the only entertainment of a public character. Every morning the officer of the day is called upon to change guard; and while this is in order, the band of the post will give the people some fine music on the plaza. The streets here are only about nine feet wide, without a side-walk, which is the most amazing sight you can see anywhere in Florida.

These streets were in time of the Spanish rule kept in excellent order; but now are badly cut up, dirty and dusty with the shifting sand.

The houses are but two stories high, with an out-reaching piazza fronting each, opening on the second floor; from the piazza on one side of the street, across to one of the houses opposite, two persons could nearly touch hands. The plan of this old city reminds one of the oldest part of the city of Quebec. Very few of the old Spanish stock are now living here; but you can detect in the bright eye, elastic step, and raven locks of some of the many pretty women, the evidence of the Spanish blood. There are two or three fair hotels; but a first-class hotel is sadly needed. A number of private boarding-houses are open, kept by estimable, educated ladies, who do all in their power to make their guests comfortable; but unfortunately for new arrivals, are always full; in fact, their apartments are engaged from year to year in advance.

Northern invalids going to St. Augustine, will find almost every available house crowded

Going South for the Winter. 57

to the utmost, with wasted desponding consumptives. The stranger who arrives here to remain the winter, *without giving previous notice*, and *securing* apartments, must expect to fare little better than at other Florida winter resorts. As to hotel management, it is just the same here at St. Augustine as you find it wherever the *season* is a short one, and hotel men must make their profits in a few short months during the year. Too often the hotels everywhere are conducted by parties entirely ignorant of the wants and necessities of their guests, who may be ill with consumption.

There will be a change for the better in the hotel accommodation at St. Augustine shortly, as enterprising parties of large experience in hotel management in New Jersey (Long Branch) are preparing to have in working order a much better hotel than has ever been known there; which will prove profitable both to the proprietors and the public. *Some* persons who are *now* satisfied, perhaps well pleased with Florida hotels, but they are either sadly uninformed of the wants, comforts and diet required by the consumptive, or are so hearty, and have so much vigor that they cannot understand why the sick and prostrate sufferer should have extra care and attention.

If parties who go to St. Augustine in search of health, can take a cottage and supply their own table, or obtain board in one of the excellent private boarding-houses, they can be assured of a most lovely winter climate, with fruit and vegetables nearly all the winter. Oranges are very plenty, and exceedingly luscious. One cannot conceive of the life and freshness of the pure, golden fruit, plucked as they hang in clusters, direct from the enormous trees. A healthy orange-tree will yield from five to ten thousand marketable oranges yearly; such trees are not unlike our mature, thrifty apple-trees, but much more compact, and inexpressibly lovely to look at, "oranges, sweet oranges," as they are floating in the bright sunlight of the sunny South. Previous to 1835, when St. Augustine was visited with the most severe frost ever known there, the income from oranges was very great. The writer met with a number of speculators from the Eastern States who had invested all their means in a wild scheme of growing oranges for the northern market, and, of course, made a bad failure; as have many cotton speculators who had entered plantations. Orange-trees are slow growers. It will be a good investment for a father to set an orange grove for his son, who, in twenty years, will have a fortune from his oranges. The best trees are twenty years of age. Such monstrous lemons are seen nowhere else, as are grown in gardens here. For those consumptive patients who can be located comfortably here for the winter, we can safely say, that there is no place in the United States equal to St. Augustine for a winter home of the invalid, who, after a trial, finds the disagreeable shortness of breath not increasing on him.

The influence of such air and such a mild climate for a person suffering from weak lungs, is marked, and the improvement often rapid and lasting; *provided*, the sick person can secure such diet and surroundings as are indispensable in the treatment of phthisis. The opportunity and inducements for exercise in the open air, with a clear, blue sky overhead, and numberless shady nooks and groves to hide in, while snuffing the pure sea-breezes ever changing, and coming to you filled with the saline emanations from the ocean, is truly grateful and profitable. The riding, driving and fishing in the midst of winter, with a beautiful sail of an afternoon over Matanzas Sound, and out of the inlet to the ocean, is something that, I believe, cannot elsewhere be indulged in with so much satisfaction and benefit to the consumptive. There are to be seen any day in winter, on Matanzas Sound, enough of pleasure boats to hire for fishing and sailing, or alligator shooting, down the coast, inland, making sufficient amusement, if only sought after.

In these statements, I only give my own experience, which is entirely impartial and honest, having no interest but the interest of those consumptives who have *no time to doubt or delay,* and who are zealously seeking daily for a

Going South for the Winter. 61

true statement of the advantages (if any) of "going South for the winter."

I wish now, to give to all such timely warning, that they must expect to endure priva--tions and vexations which *cannot* be anticipated. You must not expect to find perpetual sunshine, or equable temperature always anywhere in the South. The dampness of evening will often warn the consumptive to seek the warmth and cheer of a good fire, even in Florida; and on the damp, disagreeable days —as such occur during winter—extra caution about exposure and dress might be exercised.

In reaching St. Augustine there is one serious difficulty, and the uncertainty of getting away again, is worth mentioning.

After touching a steamboat landing on the St. John River, named Picolata (which will always be remembered by the unfortunates), consisting of a one-story building for a stage station, where the poor ghostly, colorless sufferer is left by the steamer, ready to fall from exhaustion, and fainting for breath, upon the steamboat dock, is told he must remain in this little station building, as the only shelter for the remainder of the day, and possibly with a chance of spending the night on the floor, with the best provision that can be made in the way of bedding, from this "Picolata," a very tiresome ride of eighteen miles in horribly crowded stages, is the only opportunity to get to St. Augustine. In going to and returning from there, you find the stages always over-crowded and disagreeable. The strongest passenger will always find stage seats, and over-reach the weaker who may require assistance to climb into the stages; and the consequence is, the disappointed and discouraged health-seeker is obliged to stop at this apology for a stage depot, until the next day. The weakest consumptive must submit to all sorts of extortion, imposition and impudence practiced upon him *from the moment he leaves his home.* The manner in which Northerners, far advanced in phthisis, and almost helpless, submit to be packed in stages, steamboats and so-called hotels and boarding-houses in Florida, is marvellous.

Going South for the Winter. 63

After a night at Picolata station, you rise from a bed on the floor, (which the writer was *glad to get* going and returning from St. Augustine,) after an unrefreshing rest, and, with a scanty meal, prepare for a stage ride of five hours, through sand near a foot deep, for St. Augustine. If it were *possible to know when* the sick friends would reach "Picolata" landing, by all means get word to St. Augustine for a *special* conveyance to meet the boat on arrival. The people at this "station" are very kind and sympathising, wearing themselves out to oblige the stranger, doing all they can with the very limited means provided. All efforts are, however, unavailing for the comfort of the sick; and it were far better, and, in fact the only sensible plan, to have a conveyance ready to take you across to St. Augustine direct. It is to be hoped that the irrepressible Yankee will soon open steam communication to St. Augustine, by changing the entrance to the harbor; when soundings, now only nine feet on the bar at low water, preventing the approach of able steamers, will be altered so as to admit large steamers. When this shall be accomplished, we expect to see this old town of St. Augustine the Newport of America.

ENTERPRISE.

On a lake far up the St. John river, at the head of navigation. south-east from St. Augustine, and almost hid from view by the gigantic water oak, magnolias, cypress, maple, palmetto and palm, all embraced by the characteristic moss covering, and hanging in dismal masses of gray drapery from every limb, is a landing called Enterprise. This is as far south in Florida as invalids from the North ever think of going for the winter. Here, in the midst of the great alligator nursery of the St. John, surrounded by mocking birds and stately white cranes, often startled by the scream of the bird of Washington, our imperial eagle, the consumptive can bask in the heat of the sun, (so intense as to hatch alligator eggs,) shining upon sand as white as snow, blinding one, and making exercise impossible.

Enterprise has two or three houses and a hotel, owned by the captain and owner of the steam-boat "Darlington," which brings you here from Jacksonville. Captain Brock rents his hotel to a down-easter and runs his steamboat himself. The hotel building is quite a roomy house, capable of "crowding in" say forty or fifty guests. The proprietor keeps as good a house as can be expected so far from "everywhere."

This single hotel is the only provision made to receive the worn-out, half-starved, disgusted invalid. This region is destitute of interest and comfort for the sick man, and entirely too far from home and friends to suit many who desire to winter in Florida; everything used has to be boated up the river from the North. The country does not produce anything; ice is much wished for by the sick, but must be used sparingly from the difficulty of obtaining it, while none but insane consumptives would think of asking for good ice water to drink on arriving at the landing here in the "Darlington," after a very tiresome trip up the river. If not so touching, it would be amusing to see the surprise of the strangers who crowd together looking vacantly about for the "village" of Enterprise. The place is so much talked of by healthy parties (sportsmen) on the river, that the consumptive is deceived as to the character of the place, and in consequence, may go up to Enterprise, where they find the hotel full of northerners, sent down here to die and be buried in the shifting sand. It is impossible to imagine the melancholy air, haggard, suffering, wasted form, sparkling eye, and sunken cheek of the poor creatures on the river and at all the landings, bathed in prespiration from weakness and the heat of the burning sun, parched and choked for ice and cooling drinks, wandering about dejected, disgusted with the transparent humbug of trying to gain health and strength in this barren waste, and almost ready to drop into the hideous jaws of the alligator and end their misery.

Going South for the Winter. 67

In this latitude bananas, figs, cocoa-nuts, coffee, olives, lemons, and ginger may be cultivated; and while the climate here and at Indian River and Key West, is more mild than at any other locality within the limits of the United States, I would not care to have patients select this region for the winter; but for sportsmen, who are "looking up" a place to enjoy the winter, there is no place where you can kill a breakfast of deer at easier rifle-shot without leaving your camp. The astonished deer will walk directly over your camping place. Bear, panther, and wild-cat abound in the interior of the dense forest. The weather is so mild, that the only shelter required, if you wish to lodge out-of-doors, is a simple rubber blanket, or you can suspend yourself with comfort on a hammock.

As the mosquitoes never get their wings touched with frost, they are very healthy and troublesome late in the season. For alligator shooting, this cove of Enterprise is always alive with enormous alligators, which are only driven away from the landing by the steamboat. The further you go up the lake from here, the more plenty and bold you find the alligators, and all large game. It would prove spendid sport to take a boat and paddle up the lake, fighting your way among the twenty-feet long alligators, and if your pluck will allow you to go ashore in the marsh, you can walk over acres of alligators, while shooting with the greatest ease and pleasure, as many splendid turkeys as would supply our eastern market for Thanksgiving Day.

As I am only interested in the question of climatic influences in the treatment of pulmonary consumption, I will leave others to describe the wonderful and amazingly wild scenery, and all the wonders of the St. John river. Parties who wish for *pure, unadultcrated* sport, hunting in the middle of winter, will find all the sport, and a table and accommodation suited to *their* wants, at Captain Brock's hotel, at Enterprise; but for the sick and weary consumptive, places not so far from direct and easy communication with the North should be tried first; very few feeble con

Going South for the Winter.

sumptive persons have the strength required to undertake long journeys. The trip to Enterprise is attended with difficulties, and requires more exertion and effort than most invalids can endure, who will find only apologies for the rich butter, delicious bread, fat beef, mutton, milk, and sweet cream, of special value to the sick man.

LAKE HARNEY.

Lake Harney can be visited by parties who choose to hire a little steamer kept for the purpose at this landing. The lake can be "done" in one day, and nowhere can pleasure-seekers find so much really-exciting sport, while gazing in wonder and delight upon a tropical wilderness.

Hunting parties could leave New York in winter by the quickest and most direct route, reaching Brock's hotel at Enterprise at the end of a week—allowing two weeks for shooting and another for returning—reaching home after only a month's absence, entirely surfeited with most magnificent sport.

AIKEN, SOUTH CAROLINA.

It would be impossible to find any climate *fully* equal to the necessities of the patients with pulmonary disease; but nature not interfered with, and aided by climatic influences, will often provide more wisely for the consumptive than the physician can hope to.

It must be remembered by the consumptive, that, to accomplish much, *he must himself take advantage of every circumstance and opportunity for improvnig his condition.* If he be wanting in prudence or resolution and promptitude in using *all* the means and influences he can command to make a vigorous prosecution of his "battle for life," he will miserably fail. Every individual with serious lung trouble must *feel that he is fighting for existence*, if he would be successfully treated.

Having taken a hasty view of all the points in Florida of interest to the consumptive, we

Going South for the Winter. 71

cannot do better than spend a few moments in considering the propriety of a winter in South Carolina.

About one hundred miles by rail from Charleston, you will find a pleasant village and section of country covered with lofty old pines, and an atmosphere permeated with pitch-pine perfume. This region has many special advantages of climate to recommend it as peculiarly suited to cases of pulmonary consumption. For miles around, a beautiful, wild, healthy country of hill and dale meet the eye. This whole section of South Carolina is one vast forest of noble old pines.

To reach Aiken from Charleston by rail, you will pass through horrible swampy, worthless land, suited for the great breeding-place for reptiles and insects of every variety and size. From the time you leave Charleston, the country rises gradually till you reach Aiken, six hundred feet above the level of the sea, and breathe altogether the most tonic and easily-breathed air of any locality in the South. The buoyancy of the air is at once remarked. Aiken will, undoubtedly and deservedly, be a great resort for scores of invalids from the North.

The village of Aiken is decidedly the most central and easy of access in reach of the consumptive, having regular daily mail opportunities for getting horses and carriages, *good water*, good society, with no vicious exhalations to poison the air, a clear sky and magnificent scenery, making this region very desirable as a winter residence. Aiken has four churches, a number of well-stocked country stores, pleasant private boarding-houses, post-office and fine railroad depot building.

A number of physicians are here, some being old residents and reliable practitioners; while other Eastern State physicians have, since the late war, located here for the purpose of receiving patients and treating them in their own dwellings. The old residents are highly educated, obliging and kind to strangers, treating northern people with civility In the interior, some of the inhabitants still consider a northern man their enemy, and have no confidence or communication with him; but all want quiet, and an opportunity to begin life anew, and let bygones be bygones.

The writer rode from seven to ten miles daily about the neighborhood of Aiken, during *a month in winter*, for observation and to test the climate, and does not remember ever to have received an unkind word; but, on the contrary, even when miles away, over hills covered with almost impenetrable grand old pine woods, found every stranger, horseman or hunter, communicative and agreeable."

The soil of this region of South Carolina is, much of it, unsuited to agricultural pursuits, but on the ridges is fertile and well adapted to the culture of the *grape*—an inducement for consumptives to settle here. The best land here has been offered by the owners at a ridiculously low price. Several fine farms for vineyard culture, lately owned by parties here, have been caught up by northern speculators, who purchased these valuable properties with fine buildings, often securing the whole at what it would cost to build the dwellings alone. Much of the best property has been purchased within a few months.

Up to the present time, nothing in the hotel line accommodation, really worthy of a spot where nature has lavished her treasures on, has been done. All around, the country is wild, broken and romantic. You look from your window on a chain of hills and ridges, with here and there deep ravines, watercourses and hollows, which make up the peculiar features of this healthful region, yet almost entirely deserted.

There is one large hotel at this place, where guests can be made comfortable. The sleeping-apartments are roomy, unusually so—each with a large fire-place for a pine-wood fire, furnishing a very cheering retreat on a rainy day. Every opportunity is here offered for enterprising parties to establish a "grand hotel." The private houses, always pleasant and home-like for an invalid, are full every winter, while the hotel, and buildings erected by northern physicians, who receive consumptives from the North, are crowded also.

The climate here undoubtedly offers more curative properties and advantages to the consumptive than any other locality in the South. Aiken is seldom visited by snow and severe weather—cold storms of sleet and snow so much dreaded by the invalid. The walks are always dry a *few hours* after a heavy rain, making exercise safe and profitable. The air is peculiarly dry and tonic.

The enthusiasm on breathing this stimulating atmosphere is quite enough to establish a reputation for the place. A constitution not naturally strong, is invigorated, and there is an elasticity and buoyancy of the air quite remarkable.

Exercise on horseback, so attractive and healthful, can be enjoyed without the usual extreme fatigue, and the air is just suited to the promotion and enjoyment of regular exercise; while the dry walks, covered with a flooring of pine leaves, scattered about in such profusion in the woody borders of the village, give an agreeable and pleasant variety and sensation while breathing the odor of the pine;

and those who can walk find the exercise not at all wearisome, bringing out the delightful glow of renewed health, and rousing the dormant energy of all the organs. Of course, prudence must be exercised in walking; consumptive invalids should indulge moderately, and not go into "training" for a walkist.

The thermometer does not often fall far below 32° during the winter. In December the thermometer has reached 85° as the highest and 70° the lowest. In January the highest temperature has been 75° and the lowest 40°. During the subsequent winter the highest temperature in January was 58° and lowest 48°. Although there is nothing in this region to poison the atmosphere, and apparently much to encourage the invalid; still consumptive *people die here as well as elsewhere*; even the bracing dry air of this region will revive those who reach Aiken *very much* reduced. There are some objections to this climate that the consumptive should know of.

Fabulous stories are told of sick people who arrived at Aiken, reduced to the last extremi-

Going South for the Winter. 77

ty, and whose subsequent appearance created such a surprise. The accuracy of all such reports, consumptives will be at liberty to doubt or believe. I would not have any hopeless invalid deceived by exaggerated stories, either by speculators, hotel men, or ignorant people. It is a very serious business, this going so far from home, and it very often takes all the means at hand to bear the expense; while in some cases much benefit is received by wintering in the South, other cases derive little or no benefit.

Neither would I have my readers guided by my statements, but only strive to familiarize the sick man with the locality likely to be beneficial; after which the consumptive must decide which he may do, without such an experience as the writer had in search of the section for phthisis patients to pass the winter in.

The climate of the region of country about Aiken—generally reliable—is sometimes surprisingly variable, and many who are seriously ill have sometimes to keep in-doors, with a huge pine-wood fire during morning and evening, while at noon-day they can come out and enjoy exercise, riding and driving. For those not seriously ill, a slight puff of wind from off the hills will not make them uncomfortable. At times the changes of temperature are sudden, sharp and serious, sending "all hands" flying to their quarters.

There is a scarcity of beef and milk; the cattle of the country are roaming at will, with no protector or provider, till wanted for slaughter, and never fed or housed, but forced to get a scanty subsistence from the brush, leaves, and a tuft of wild grass here and there in the forest and along the roads. Such provender will not make good milk or beef. The only plan, if milk cannot be purchased, is to persuade some one to "put up" their cow and feed the animal, selling you the milk unskimmed; or hire one of the creatures and furnish her with good fodder. A good goat can be had that will give about as much milk as many of the cows. The cows here are the most miserable specimens in the world; very small

Going South for the Winter. 79

and only equalled in starved appearance by the swine of the country.

A party who suffers from lung diseases, but having plenty of means to provide a good diet and luxuries for his comfort, can live at Aiken all winter with great satisfaction, if he chooses to pay well for extras. The village being only twelve miles from Augusta, Georgia, an invalid with means can purchase extras and necessary articles of convenience and diet, having all sent daily to him from Augusta.

Parties of four or five, who wish to club together and live apart from the hotel, can rent a house, furnishing their table for the winter months with daily supplies from Augusta. There is a medicinal spring here which is of no particular account to the consumptive, but which will be bottled up for New York before long, no doubt.

In selecting a room at the hotel at Aiken, or other resort, choose one on the second floor, where the sun will shine directly through your window during the greater part of the day, and as large a room as possible, with an open fire-place, and a free circulation of air. After a winter judiciously spent at Aiken or Augustine, with unremitting attention to the instructions of their physician, I can see no reason (provided nutritious, strong, rich, hearty food can be had) why consumptives should not return home presenting signs of permanent improvement.

SOUTH OF FRANCE.

No one, I imagine, who can have paid much attention to the treatment of pulmonary phthisis would advise a consumptive to leave the "Sunny South" of the United States for a winter residence on the shore of the Mediterranean. Dr. Henry Bennet (whose authority on such cases is the best in Europe) says that the warmth and sunshine which the consumptive can enjoy during the winter months in the climate of the French Mediterranean, is equal almost to the warmth and brightness of the British summer.

This is gratifying to those consumptives whose home is in London or Paris, and we will not doubt of the beneficial effects of such a genial climate for those who are within a reasonable distance of such latitude, and who can reach the Mediterranean region without the risk of being struck down with violent hemorrhage from over exertion and exposure on the way. If we admit that pulmonary phthisis is a disease of debility and organic exhaustion, what folly it is for the consumptive of America to exhaust his little remaining strength in knocking about his berth on a twelve-days' sea voyage with prostrating seasickness and subsequent waste of strength, in the vain endeavor to reach Madeira or Mentone. Even if after a wearisome sea voyage, the consumptive should arrive at Havre, it is not at all probable that the diet and lodging would be suited to his case; while the dangerous excitement, constant, tiresome, nervous gazing at the changing scenes, and the European manner of living in apartments, often four and five floors up from the street, make it impossible for any one subject to hemorrhages of the lungs to live with safety.

The wintering places of the South of France, which have proved beneficial for pulmonary invalids, are many, but of no interest to the consumptives of America, who should not exhaust the small allowance of vitality by the anxiety and effort to "keep up" on a European tour. In the case of the consumptive who can have little hope of recovery, for the reason that he will not take the needful care of himself, the only place for such an one is at home, where he can receive fresh instructions from his physicians daily, as new complications arise, and where he will not run the risk of a death-bed among strangers in a strange land. The pulmonary invalid should never think of leaving his native land to cross the ocean, either in the earlier or the advanced stage of the disease, unless one can be assured of unusual advantages, such as can only be provided by an extravagant expenditure of money.

DIET.

We all understand that food introduced into the mouth is there crushed, mingled with saliva, and passed on into the stomach, where by action of the secretions, it becomes pulp, and is ready to make blood, support and nourish the body, while depositing fat in one part and flesh in another.

There can hardly be a limitation in the quantity and quality of food *positively* necessary to supply material for the unceasing change and waste wearing out the consumptive patient. The nature and efficacy of food in these cases is of the greatest possible importance, and there must be no economy so-called practical in selecting a diet; the richest, most nutritious and pleasing to the palate, must be had *at whatever cost. There is no alternative, the consumptive must eat.* Before eating food, the question the sufferer with pulmonary consumption should answer, is: "Will this food form fat?" Eat only such food as will make you plump and rubicund; and eat with careful consideration, for the after-labor of the digestive apparatus, giving the stomach no unnecessary work by eating innutritious food. Consumptive persons may have four or five meals a day—breakfast, luncheon, dinner, tea and supper.

The various articles of diet differ so materially in the amount of nutritive matter, that it is essential the consumptive *should know* of the diet best calculated to promote nutrition; while the digestibility of the food must be considered a necessary part of its nutritive value. It would be well if the consumptive would be dieted by his physician, who has an accurate acquaintance with quantity, quality and efficacy of food beneficial for such patients. Diabetes, diarrhea, dyspepsia, dropsy and other complications, will indicate the variety, and modify or increase the allowance. In choosing a diet, the invalid must consult the immediate requirements of the body, as well as the circumstances of climate, peculiar employment, harassing, mental or physical labor, blood-making power, exposure, active exercise, perfect or imperfect mastication, sedentary habit, age, temperament, and particularly the condition of the digestive apparatus. The dietary must be fitted to the constitutional wants of *each* individual.

In some consumptive people, digestion is slow; in other cases, rapid. In some, a very little excitement or exertion before a meal is enough to banish one's appetite for consequent fretfulness and want of appetite during the day. A particular variety of diet is found insupportable by some consumptives, while exactly suited to the other. Veal (meat) acts almost as a poison when eaten by some, producing violent vomiting and diarrhea. The most easily digested meats cannot be tolerated by one person, which, for another, is very proper. A selected diet will rapidly make blood for one consumptive, which, for another, will need artificial assistance.

Persons who are suffering with pulmonary consumption, have always a predisposition to digestive derangements and bowel affections, in consequence of which great care must be exercised in selecting a nutritious aliment, which, while soothing to the irritable mucous membrane, have sufficient strength in its composition, besides being stimulating, palatable and supporting in its character.

There is, in all cases of consumption, a complete breaking down of the constitution, and want of proper nutriment increases the difficulty. All diseases of a tuberculous and scrofulous character are never mitigated by the patient subjecting himself to a simple regime. All the evidence and knowledge we possess of the character of this disease (phthisis), point unmistakably to a want of suitable diet, as one of the active causes of the disease.

The erroneous notion that a vegetarian diet will support a man in health and strength is a terrible mistake. The wear of the mental, muscular and nervous functions, waste of tissue, and constant work of the viscera, and all the processes undergoing continual wear, even in a healthy man, require an abundant supply of nutriment to repair the loss; and surely the consumptive must have an *active, restoring diet.*

The consumptive must bear in mind that a *strong* diet is worth everything in the treatment of his disease; and *the first* in the list of articles of diet for the phthisis patient is *cod liver oil*, without which food the progress of the disease will be checked slowly. This *indispensable food* for the consumptive can always be had at home or abroad, and *never fails* to show its wonderful effects when properly and regularly used.

The Egyptians instructed their kings, and prescribed by law, the quantity and quality of their food.

Achilles was bred for a hero, and, it is said, they fed him on the marrow of lions. Galen lived to the age of one hundred and forty, and was never ill till his last moments. His diet consisted always of strong and hearty food; he considered lettuce as having a sedative effect, and used it freely for the last meal of the day. Thomas Parr, a farmer, who lived much in the open air, was a strong feeder, and married when he was one hundred and twenty years of age.

We have numerous instances of men living one hundred and twenty, and over one hundred and twenty-eight, who were, from necessity, strong livers; and we all have heard of the Philadelphia shoemaker, who lived upon the most hearty food, and reached the age of one hundred and fourteen years. It is recorded of an English fisherman, who, at one hundred years of age, could swim equal to the smartest boy, his diet being often oatmeal and butter-milk. He died after living one hundred and sixty-nine years.

All of these hearty, long-lived people made eating an *important business* of the day, and were unlike our devotees of fashion, who exhibit so much fashionable affectation and mincing at meals as to endanger their health.

Cases of pulmonary consumption are almost entirely unknown among a class of South Americans who live on *beef*. Sir Francis Head says, in his " Notes," " That when he first crossed the Pampas—although accustomed to riding horseback all his life—he could not at all ride with the natives, who lived on beef and water alone." " But," says Sir Francis, "after I had lived on *beef* and water for a month, I found myself in a condition which I can only describe by saying, that I felt no exertion could kill me. For weeks," he says, " he would be upon his horse before sunrise, and ride until three hours after sunset, and really tired out twelve horses." This, he states, he could only have done while living on *beef*.

The ruinous broth-diet-system is to be avoided by the consumptive, and only such food allowed as will contribute to the formation of fat.

Milk is of the utmost importance, and must not be used sparingly. Goat's milk is to be preferred to that drawn from the cow. Milk diet for the consumptive cannot be too highly appreciated. Cow's milk, when pure, should be of a yellowish-white color; its specific gravity varies between 1.032 and 1.035. Mare's milk is white in color, thick, like goat's milk;

contains a large amount of fat and sugar of milk. Asses' milk is perfectly white, and much sweeter than cow's milk, and rich in sugar of milk. Milk is classed among the most easily digested articles of food, two hours being the time required for its digestion. Woman's milk is more quickly digested than any known. Goat's milk will not make butter or take on cream. Sheep's milk will make butter, which cannot be used. Cow's milk is the most easily procured and generally used; but none but that drawn from *young, healthy animals* should be used. Goat's milk, used medicinally, may be diluted at the first using, to divest it of its peculiar taste, till the stomach becomes accustomed to it. The importance of some discipline and good order in the management of the dining-room is worth reasonable attention; and, for the consumptive, it is absolutely necessary to leave all melancholy feelings and reflections "outside" at meal-time. Eat slow, talk slow, and never bring your cares, or allow others to offer their troubles for discussion, at the table in the dining-room. Never permit any but cheerful conversation. Select for associates the most easy, natural and perfect characters, who will enliven and warm you through-and-through by their boisterous hilarity, rollicking fun and round-ringing laughter. Such companions, full of sympathy, kind in heart and pure in life, will drive all anxiety and dread of death from pulmonary consumption from your mind.

"A merry heart doeth good like a medicine, but a broken spirit drieth the bones."—PROVERBS xvii. 22.

EXERCISE.

It is the most preposterous nonsense to suppose, that after having forced upon yourself evident physical degeneracy by a merciless application to business or excessive mental activity, with the usual starvation diet — taxing body and mind to such a degree as actually to produce the most disastrous results — to suppose, we say, that your enfeebled stomach, loss of appetite, poverty of blood, failing sight, labored action of the heart, sluggish circulation — really having transgressed all the laws of health, bereft of nerve and vigor, that you can, by a few days' bodily exercise, overcome your depressed condition, arrest the destruction of tissue, and regain health and strength!

For those consumptives who have such extravagant notions regarding the value of exercise, we can refer them to the decrees of the great lawgiver Lycurgus, in his ordinances for the physical training of his people. Lycurgus decreed that all the virgins should exercise themselves in running, wrestling, jumping and quoits, and thus fortified by this exercise, their bodies might be strong and vigorous, and their children the same; and, in order to extinguish the delicacy of the sex, Lycurgus ordered them, on certain festivals, to appear nude and dance, going through running and wrestling exercises; and the young men were ordered to go nearly naked on these festive occasions and join in the dance. All this was witnessed by the king and senate. The young men were praised by the multitude for their bravery, and the virgins celebrated for their great strength, while everything was conducted with modesty and without anything disgraceful in it. The young maidens, we are told, became very strong and brave women, which is seen by the words of the wife of Leonidas, when another woman from a far country said to her, "You of Lacedæmon are the only women in the world that rule the men;" she answered, "We are the only women that bring forth men."

To encourage this sort of exercise, and these public wrestlings and dances, in which we are asked to believe there was always good order and decorum observed, a punishment was put upon all those who would insist on being unmarried and wished to continue single; for by Lycurgus's law the time of marriage *was fixed*. The would-be bachelors were commanded, on these festive occasions, to march naked round the market-place, and, for their disobedience of the law, were not permitted to join in the exercises. Now, here in the decrees of one of the most remarkable men who ever lived, we see to what extremes men will go in their enthu-, siasm. It is said history repeats itself; we should hope "not so" of Lycurgus's history. Out-of-door exercise, if had in *moderation*, is conducive to an improved condition of the consumptive invalid, and may be recommended as a necessary part of the treatment of phthisis; but we desire to impress earnestly upon the consumptive, the fact that exercise carried beyond reason, is the immediate cause of hemorrhage, and attended with the greatest danger. It is for the consumptive to judge of the needful exercise by prudent experiment.

The moment one feels tired, *stop*. You cannot, after the least sign of weariness, continue to exercise safely; then you will be obtaining your experimental knowledge at too great hazard; and you must respect the warning of nature, and try your strength no further, unless you are prepared to bring upon yourself additional trouble.

Regularity of exercise, when the weather

permits, with the express purpose, and a general bearing upon the object in view, certainly is beneficial, increasing the expansion of the lungs. The breathing becomes more deep and full, and the fresh air, a constant stimulant, is respired with pure oxygen, giving renewed energy and power to the vital organs.

In active or passive exercise, walking or riding in the open air, you escape from the heated, foul air which you constantly breathe in-doors, and which is unfit for respiration. Exercise, while inhaling confined air, will be of little service to the consumptive, as there can be, in such atmosphere, no healthy action of the lungs, while the increasing perspiration, exhalations from the body and particles of fine dust from the floor and carpeting of the room, always floating about, added to the noxious gases of the close apartment, only produce an entire loss of energy and appetite. The necessity for regular exercise, passive or active, being admitted, it then becomes a question for the consumptive, *where and when* exercise can be had with the most profit?

Where, from the elevation of the surrounding country the air is pure, dry and easily breathed, is evidently most desirable. Having a choice, the consumptive would, undoubtedly, select for active exercise the air of a mountainous region; but, unfortunately for the sufferer, such a salubrious locality cannot be had at pleasure, with the means at command of many who need to breathe and exercise in such an atmosphere. Then the question arises, can any of the schemes proposed by the gymnasium afford the desired exercise for the consumptive who must remain in a crowded city? All gymnasium exercises in necessarily poorly-ventilated rooms, are subject to difficulties, which interfere much with the natural functions.

We will not doubt that exercise in the gymnasium, for those who prefer such violent exercise—jumping and lifting and the dumb-bells—is suited; still, for *anyone*, there can be no particular advantage in developing one class of muscles by great muscular exertion for which the whole system must suffer; and *the hour selected* for gymnastic exercise is one, of all others, the least to be desired.

After a busy day in the office or on the street—and often the nervous energy and vitality is almost expended—it seems a poor time to exert oneself in jumping and dragging exercise, in the vitiated air of fifty gas burners, while stealing from Nature the hours demanded for relaxation and physical rest. The consumptive must select the variety of exercise in which the movements are best calculated to expand the chest. For those invalids with phthisis, who go to Florida, *rowing* exercise (on Matanzas sound or St. John river) is *the best* possible form. The exercises which bring into play the muscles of the upper extremities are the most proper for the consumptive. The arms must be actively employed as well as the legs, not in lifting, but backward and forward movements, such as pulling a boat, thereby expanding the chest.

STIMULANTS.

Some over-zealous, but good honest men have in their surpassing goodness opened a crusade upon the physicians who will use as a medicine any alcoholic stimulant. If it were not such a serious matter, it would be very' amusing to hear these constitutionally robust men. They know nothing of the concealed cares, troubles, anxiety, worry and vexation of the weakly, almost prostrate, women who are mentally and physically tired out with the every-day annoyances and hubbub of the "servants of the period," whose ignorance is enough to give any housekeeper the hysterics, and despair of all success in domestic management; and shall these praiseworthy men, who are never ill, (and who have their convenient club-house, quiet rare-bit, mug of ale and sweet forgetfulness,) expect the physician to look on unmoved without using every means in his power to avert the danger from continued prostration threatening his consumptive patient.

Every right minded man in the profession is anxious to see the temperance cause advance; and in their capacity do full as much for the cause as those, who are so ready to censure the physician. No regular practitioner, who intelligently understands the cause and cure of consumption, will be willing to deny his patient with chronic lung disease either good Burton ale, champagne or brandy, with his cod-liver oil.

Do the robust, hearty men, who know nothing of the pain and suffering of the pulmonary invalid, expect the physician to look on without the most energetic effort to stay the disease which threatens the life of the consumptive patient? And will they tell us that in cases of extreme suffering and exhaustion, we shall not make cautious use of stimulants, which in moderation the patient undoubtedly requires?

This is "all bosh," and the most dangerous folly, for which we can have no patience to discuss with the temperance men, who *injure* the cause by their intemperate struggle to compel every one to accord with their designs. In Captain Bligh's account of the sufferings of himself and companions, in consequence of the mutiny of the crew of his ship, he remarks, "the little rum we had was of great service, when our nights were particularly distressing."

Sir John Ross says, in his Arctic Expedition, that when experimenting upon the men of two boats' crews, rowing in a heavy sea, the water-drinkers would outdo the men who had an allowance of grog; so that the physician must take the responsibility, without regard to any outside influences; *he alone* is responsible for the medical treatment of his patient. The most reviving and active stimulant within the reach of all consumptives is music. Not without reason did Lord Holland treat his horses to a regular weekly concert in the stable, on the plea that music cheered their hearts and modified their temper.

The influence of sun-light on our pulmonary invalid is really most surprising, and is a powerful stimulant, that should be sought for by all consumptives.

SEA-BATHING.

The writer has had an experience of many years in sea-water bathing on the coast, and does not hesitate to express a firm belief in the healing properties of sea-water, particularly for nervous, over-worked females, with cold extremities, (who will obtain the most striking and remarkable results from judicious bathing in the ocean). The value of sea-bathing in the treatment of phthisis is not often over-estimated. Sea-water is supposed to contain in its composition a minute quantity of sulphates of soda and lime, with bromine and iodine. To be most effectual, sea-water baths should be taken at some point on the coast, and out-of-doors. The action of the air upon the bather having considerable influence for good. The time selected should be at noon-day, before eating. After coming out, have a milk-punch or glass of wine and an hour for rest before eating.

The consumptive may remain in the water

five minutes at first, increasing the time to ten minutes. There must be no fighting the wind and waves, but gentle dipping under water only. The water should be pleasantly warm before entering. When "going in," walk from the beach rapidly till you are covered to the arm-pit, and then dive under. There is danger in a dash or hurried plunge into the surf, on account of the severe shock which has sometimes proved very serious for the consumptive. The bather must be governed much by his own feelings, unless directly under the care of a physician. One can judge of the good or ill effects of sea-water bathing by the sensation after coming out. If after reaching the bathing-house the skin has a red and warm look, and there be a feeling of renewed vigor and a general stimulated sensation, that will be positive evidence that the bath has produced good effects. If, on the contrary, there is a slight cough and chilly feeling, a want of glow, and the skin have a cold, rough appearance, the bath should not be repeated, unless by the advice of the physician.

CONCLUSION.

One of the great dangers the consumptive has to guard against, is the flattering character of the disease. Very many pulmonary patients lose all they may have gained by judicious treatment, by their over-confidence and consequent risk and exposure during bad weather. Those consumptives who should remain at home and in bed, are too often persuaded by the flattering but deceitful signs of improvement, to believe that exposure and breathing a cold and raw atmosphere will not be so serious as the physician insists that it will prove.

Consumptive invalids who have recovered rapidly, often forget that they must *continue to fight* the disease. Permanent relief can only be secured by constant watchfulness, protection from atmospheric vicissitudes, and everything that may increase the lowered vitality.

While I would earnestly recommend for persons suffering from pulmonary phthisis.

both the grape and the milk cure (particularly the milk treatment), yet these must not be relied on for replacing the cod liver oil. It is to be remembered that the disease wearing out the consumptive is a constitutional as well as local disorder, and everything that can improve and maintain the highest condition of bodily vigor, is to be eagerly sought for; while at the same time guarding against all reducing medicines and starvation diet. From the very commencement of the disease, the invalid must consider himself in the greatest danger, and early devote his time and money to re-establishing his health.

Immediate active and energetic treatment will often prevent further advance of the disease. The influence of hygienic and climatic treatment in retarding the progress of the disease, is admitted by all who have studied the character of phthisis.

The wearisome cough must be quieted, and hemorrhages checked in the beginning. The continuous, slow fever consuming the consumptive must be watched, and the rapid loss of strength, appetite, and general "wasting away," as well as troublesome diarrhea, must be provided for; stimulants should be given, and, where indicated, brandy and ammonia. Consumptives must be *made to take food.* Too great quantities, and at irregular intervals, may derange the functions of the stomach; but care can be exercised. At all events, the invalid consumptive *must* be made to eat.

The manner in which the nurse administers nourishment to the invalid will often banish his appetite. A pleasant, well-meaning and unaffected nurse is a valuable aid in the treatment of consumptives.

The nurse should be cautioned not to approach a patient as if expecting him to devour everything with a relish. A teaspoonful of this, a forkful of the other, a little jelly and a bit of toast at will, is far better than the obtrusive manner of a nurse who will insist on selecting the cuts herself. All the little morsels that are a rarity and a surprise to the invalid, will often excite an appetite which has entirely fled from the call of the sufferer. Wear always flannel next the skin, winter and summer. Keep the pores of the skin open by frequent washings, which will leave the skin free to perform its functions.

After much special study and careful observation of the peculiar character of this dreaded disease, and after having repeatedly seen the marvellous results of good treatment, the writer has become a believer in the curability of pulmonary phthisis, or rather that with the influence of climate, judicious advice, sufficient rest and repose, agreeable stimulants— all such as affect through sight, hearing, smell and taste, as well as an allowance of strong beer, plentiful use of nourishing soups, oatmeal, beef, mutton, cod liver oil, cream, eggs, with entertaining society, music, and living, if possible, much in the open air, with the positive influence of sunlight and proper administration of medicines—the disease may be entirely controlled and its further progress permanently checked. Much, *very much*, can be done at home to control the disease without " GOING SOUTH FOR THE WINTER."

www.ingramcontent.com/pod-product-compliance
Lightning Source LLC
Chambersburg PA
CBHW020150170426
43199CB00010B/968